Oh, Engineering! Oh, how you do frustrate me! (In haiku format)

Pip Merryweather

This book is not a work of fiction. The characters and incidents portrayed in it are not exaggerated. Any resemblance to actual persons, living or dead, or events or localities is accurate.

Paperback Edition March 9, 2021
ISBN 978-1-78808-169-6

PREFACE

I'd like to thank you all for purchasing my book. It means a lot to me that you decided that it was worth spending some of your hard earned money on my book of Engineering Haiku. To be honest, even if you've stolen my book from somewhere, or illegally downloaded it; I'm pretty stoked that you went to that kind of effort. In fact, I'd consider it an honour that someone thought my book was good enough to risk a misdemeanor in the form of petty theft, or to make available on the internet. Regardless; however you obtained my book, I'm glad you have it and I'm grateful that you're taking the time to read it. I hope you enjoy.

Acknowledgements

I'd like to acknowledge my family, who put up with my incessant work-related moaning.

I'd also like to acknowledge my place of work. Without which I would be unable to support my family; and without which, it would not be possible to have written a book on this particular subject matter.

Contents

01

An Introduction, of Sorts

A good day to you!
This is my book of Haiku.
I hope you like it.

02

A Longer Introduction

I'll put this as politely and respectfully as possible; I do not enjoy my job[1]. You may come to realize this yourself by the end of this book. Or, you may not. I guess it all depends on how well I put across my emotions. Hopefully, I've managed to capture a sense of the frustration involved, and I haven't just come across as a whiny little engineer.

Chances are, if you're reading this book, you probably have some sort of vague understanding of what Haiku is. But, chances are, now that I've made an assumption; my assumption is probably wrong. Therefore, please allow me to briefly discuss the concept of Haiku. In this book, Haiku are simply 3 lined poems following the 5, 7, 5 syllabic structure. However, looking into Haiku in more detail, I've found that,

[1]Pssst... If you want to skip straight to the Haiku (I don't blame you, and I won't think less of you), head to Chapter 03.

apparently, there's much more complicated rules at work. But, that's out-with the scope of this, perhaps simplistic, book. Constructing something coherent and meaningful that conveys a specific intended subject or dialogue out of a mere 17 syllables is something I have found to be challenging and fun. It's almost like plugging gaps in a wall using bricks of varying length that each have a word on them. This book is a book of these walls that I've built in my mind as I mentally attempt to brick up every entrance to my workplace. Most of these Haiku are about particularly frustrating moments in my career as an Engineer; as such, this book started off as me amusing myself at my workstation, venting my frustration. But, at some point in time, things got way out of hand, and here we are now.

Anyway, since you're going to be reading some Haiku I've written about experiences in my job, I figure I should tell you a bit about myself. The accuracy of the following cannot be guaranteed:

I'm employed as a Something Engineer for a *very small* company that is **completely unheard of** in the world of Engineering. I may (or may not, bear-in-mind) live in the world's most average, or atypical city (or village), and work at the pole of inaccessibility in a small, hollow, concrete torus devoid of sunlight and atop a mighty octopus.

You would be forgiven for thinking that a company of $\pi \pm 10\%$ employees, located in such a highly accessible location could not possibly be in the business of designing and building FPSOs and Children's Play Parks; but, that's exactly what we may, or may not, do.

Whilst this attempt at misdirection may (or, may not) have gotten completely (or, not even remotely) out of hand, certain underlying truths are still present (or, completely absent);

1. I am a living person at the time this book is being written.
2. I am employed as an Engineer, of some description.
3. I'm even part of a Professional Engineering Institution.
4. I am employed by a company.
5. I wrote a book of Haiku, venting the frustration created by my job.
6. I don't enjoy my job.

But, without any further delay, I invite you to read through my Haiku.

03

An Engineering Story

Here we begin with some Haiku. This chapter tells a story, and each Haiku flows into the next, meandering their way along the perilous path that I followed in my Engineering career. It begins as it should, on the first day of my Engineering career.

I was enthusiastic on my first day. I was ready to solve any and every problem that came my way. I thought, "This is a job I'm going to enjoy; lots of engineering and problem solving."

My ID Photo.
It was taken the first day.
It's so full of hope.

I was going to revolutionise this field. I was going to invent new things, design new products. I was going to improve current products. I was going to learn all the things. I was going to research all the other things. I was going to be digging into a mountain of engineering.

And then, the illusion was shattered. There was no engineering present in that cold, gray, concrete building except the part that no one really liked; Quality Control. My ID card was updated four and a half years later, when an external photographer was hired to make our ID cards "more fun."

ID Updated.
Hair Shorter, Beard Longer; and...
The hope is now gone.

I had hoped that this new ID portrait would become my ID card of Dorian Gray, preventing myself from degrading any further. But, alas, it was not the case. I continued to fall into despair whilst my ID card retained it's 'still-containing-some-semblance-of-hope' nature.

Eventually you wise up, and you realise that no-one should be enthusiastic, lest their illusion comes crashing down, and takes everyone with them.

Enthusiasm.
It's not allowed in these halls.
Leave it at the door.

Perhaps we should put up a sign outside our premises; "Management is not responsible for any loss of hope or any damage to the psychological well-being of any person on this property."

Although, after a while, you find it somewhat encouraging when you realise that you're not the only one who has lost all hope.

"Disillusionment"
Is the company's motto.
All suffer from it.

In my case, I found that *literally everyone* in a non-managerial position in my department were despairing, and seeking alternative employment! Which, really, says a lot.

I've often thought about how amusing it'd be if company slogans were honest. It'd be interesting to see a list of companies with their official slogans/taglines alongside their unofficial slogans/taglines that truly depict the company and how it views/treats it's employees. Here's ours in Haiku format.

Employees Valued
(But just during interviews,
And company[1] website).

Come to think of it, I'd be absolutely ecstatic to hear of any unofficial company slogans that you come up with (they don't even have to be Haiku)[2]. Don't worry, I won't tell your company; I'm bound by a strict code of ethics by my professional institution.

[1]This isn't a cop-out, I promise I pronounce 'company' in two syllables

[2]Submit them on pipmerryweather.wordpress.com

On the subject of honesty. Sometimes it's very easy to tell if someone's lying. I've come to discover an important and accurate rule that I can follow to tell if management are lying.

How'd I know you'd lied?
Because your face was moving
It's obvious, sir.

You'd think that, with all the practice they're getting, they'd be able to conceal it better. Then again, maybe they want you to know they're lying to your face. Or, maybe I'm just cynical?[3]

[3] It's probably this

Interestingly, I'd like to share with you the first lie they ever told me. Way back in time, right back to my interview.

In my interview.
You said "Lots of research done"
Biggest lie ever...

I believe that 'Start as you mean to go on' is the appropriate idiom to be used at this juncture.

But, sometimes, it can be hard to tell if someone's lying. Especially if the person is a highly skilled bureaucrat. However, I've come to realise who these people are within my specific organisation; at which point, the previous rule of thumb applies.

Your words, they sound good.
But you don't really mean it.
Bureaucracy, y'all.

Ugh, *shudder*, Bureaucracy and internal politics...

Speaking of bureaucracy and management; our management have some pretty effective methods that are employed to motivate their underlings. Unfortunately, though they may be effective, it is not pleasant to be on the receiving end.

Management Lesson:
Patronisation, Blackmail;
They're the tools in here.

I wonder if there's a training course somewhere to teach me the secrets of this wonderful method of management?

Another skill shown by our management that I'd love to learn is the elegant and deeply thought through method of delegation that they employ.

"Look into this." "Why?"
"Because I can't be bothered"
Skilled Delegation...

In that case, I am glad that you consider me perfectly suited to this task.

Also, I really respect how my management view their underlings. Their method of giving feedback is an inspiration, and motivates me to strive to become a better person.

Bi-yearly assessed.
And graded from 1 to 10.
Where 10 is the worst.

Whilst I do realise that the end of the grading scale chosen to be the positive result is an arbitrary concept, it doesn't feel particularly rewarding to be judged on a scale of 'least not good' to 'most not good'; it means that you're not 'excellent', just 'very not awful'.

Although, I'm glad that management can occasionally be honest with me;

Bi-annual review:
"You are a disappointment
of highest order"

Thank you, Sir. I'm glad we had this discussion. Your in-depth feedback, along with your non-existent possible points of improvement are very helpful; I look forward to my next feedback session.

At the very least, unhelpful feedback is more helpful than no feedback at all. Sometimes, there's none to be found.

Define "Bi-Annual"
"Twice a year, or every two.
At my discretion"

This is actually one of the things that I've always respected about management. They always find a way to use vague word choice and double meanings to their advantage.

And then everything just sort of adds up, the disillusionment sets in again, and you sit down and say;

I thought, “Engineer.
I think that’ll be a fun job”
Oh, how I was wrong!

But, at least there’s still the hope that, due to the vastness of the world of Engineering, there must be some place that’s pleasant and interesting to work in. Mustn’t there?

There must be! And, I must find it.

Sun shines, and grass grows.
The birds learn to fly away.
I need a new job...

Therefore, I'll install every job search application under the sun, and receive countless alerts every day. I'll trawl through thousands of job postings, I'll print ream upon ream of copies of my CV. Or, I'll maybe just moan about it in a book of Haiku...

04

On my Interactions with Management

This chapter is dedicated solely to those who lead our respective organizations through the through the weird and wonderful world that is business and commerce (and some Engineering). They are our management.

Don't get me wrong, deadlines are fine. I can work with deadlines.

"Your report is late.
I won't check it for 10 months.
But I need it now."

But, what I can't stand is arbitrary deadlines for unimportant work that will sit unchecked until the end of time. What invariably follows is that I'll get reprimanded not continually harassing management until they've approved the work.

This is a recurring theme within my engineering career. A member of management will come to me and request that I send an email, as they do not have the time.

"I'm too important!
Write this email that I wrote!"
"Why me?" "You're nothing"

11 times out of 10, they will discuss the content and purpose of the email with me, then sit down at their desk, write out the exact email they want emailed, email it to me, and ask via email that I email their email via email. So, as per their email request, I email their emailed email via the email client to the client to be emailed the email. A fantastic waste of everyone's time. Especially when I could've used the time to write additional (or, better quality) Haiku, and given you all much greater value for money. Thanks, Management...

This is another recurring theme within my management interaction. We're having an important discussion, and I'm probably going to have to stay late to complete follow up work from the meeting. And, the phone rings...

Big work discussion.
The phone rings; boss answers it
It's his wife. Aaaaaaaaaaaand
wait...

And I wait. And I wait. And I wait. And I've to stay even later. Hooray for management and their personal intrusions.

As an interesting aside, the previous Haiku raises another wonderful feature of management. The double standard.

If my wife phoned me.
I'd be breaching policy.
Double Standards, y'all.

"You cannot do this. But I can." "Why?" "I have decreed it, my dear underling! You would do well not to question it, or I shall have no choice but to severely discipline you for a minor breach of an arbitrary rule that applies only to such lowly people as yourself."

Unsurprisingly, I don't particularly enjoy being threatened, and It's not the kind of behaviour I expect from my manager. But can happen; and it has happened. One was not amused.

"I can't work abroad."
"Fine, unemployment for you."
"I can work abroad."

Needless to say, I ended up working in a different country for an extended period of time.

The ability to prioritize work is a very important skill, one which I haven't perfected yet (by a long way). So, occasionally, I'll ask my manager for their assistance in prioritizing my work. For example; which of these tasks would you like done first?

"Which job to do first?"
"All of them, and none of them."
"Very helpful, thanks..."

The advice that I get is never helpful, and is usually along the lines of "All jobs are of highest priority, and all must be completed first."

Whilst I'm not going to complain about my pay, as I'm incredibly appreciative of the fact that it allows me to support my family. There *is* a related subject that I'd like to approach.

Must stay two more hours.
But we won't pay you for them.
It's the way of things.

Let e get this straight, it's the 21st century, and you won't pay me for the overtime that you contractually require from me? Not even time in lieu? I'm genuinely surprised that you don't also fine me an administration fee for putting additional hours on my timesheet.

Somewhat related to the previous Haiku, some managers have this wonderful ability to blissfully ignore how long any task will take. They then use their previously discussed management tools to make you work faster and longer.

"Test on-site next week."
"But, the system doesn't work."
"You will make it work."

Hooray for company culture, and for attempting to meet unrealistic and uninformed deadlines through use of passive aggressive threats, fake optimism and disingenuous encouragement. "You will make it work. I believe in you." "Why, thank you, sir! I only needed to know that you believed in me. The system will definitely work on Monday, it's just like Santa's Sleigh!"

05

On My Role within Engineering

I have never seen a job description for my current role. I'm led to believe that one exists, but I'm not allowed to see it. This section is based around my role; as if my job description was written in a series of Haiku.

I'm going to go out on a limb and say that you've probably guessed that I don't find my job terribly exciting.

What kind Engineer?
The most bored kind of all.
Administrative...

Such a guess would be correct.

Sorry for this Haiku of mine, I understand they should not rhyme. This, however, was too much fun; I'm sure that you can bear just one.

"You there, Engineer!
Move this box from there to here.
Good, good. There's a dear."

Most exciting tasks I've had this year have been moving stock from there to here. But, the second part I cannot bear; when I must replace from here to there...

Speaking of odd-jobs, I like to think of myself as a highly specialized specialist, but not in the conventional sense i.e. I'm not a Computational Magnetohydrodynamics Engineer.

Engineering niche?
I think of myself as an...
Odd-Job Engineer.

However, I am highly specialised in the execution of odd-jobs.

I'm considering getting a name badge engraved for myself, and perhaps starting a professional engineering institution.

Odd-Job Engineer.
Now my unofficial title.
Perfect Description.

Pip Merryweather MIoOJE (Member of the Institute of Odd-Job Engineers), Odd-Job Engineer.

An interesting result of my odd-job workload is that very few of my hours are actually billable.

"Please describe yourself
In one solitary word."
"I'm unbillable."

It's a wonder I haven't been released from my duty. Also, I'm sorry I lied about that being interesting, I was just trying to engage your enthusiasm.

Speaking of interesting; anything more complicated and interesting than arithmetic and basic algebra is prohibited within our building.

"Can I do some maths?"
"No, you are an Engineer,
You must do QC."

It makes me sad.

When you have slow periods at work, how do you occupy your time? I use mine productively.

No work for me now.
Must use time productively.
Writes book of Haiku.

I have to admit, it's pretty productive; I consider it "Engineering Outreach"

I should learn not to ask to go home if there's no work. There's, allegedly, always something to do.

"There's no work for you"
"Sir, may I go home then, please?"
"No, you can clean floors[1]!"

Apparently, it does not have to be engineering-related.

[1]And, once you're finished, you may remove weeds from the landscaping!

The following Haiku may sound like I'm starting to make things up.

There is no work here.
So, my boss broke a few things.
And made me fix them...

But, I assure you that this happened. Manageering, y'all.

It has occurred to me recently, that I may not actually have an engineering career.

This is no career.
This is a series of jobs.
That have no meaning.

An engineering career would have engineering jobs and professional development, right?

06

On the Subject of Professional Development

Professional Development is an incredibly important aspect of every career, and should never stop. Although, sometimes it may stop and other times it may not have started in the first place; and that's where Newton's laws of professional development came from.

I became genuinely alarmed at how quickly I was writing Haiku (I guess the frustration was venting pretty fast)

This book progresses.
Unlike my career and skills.
Let's hope the book sells...

This was the 127th Haiku that I wrote. The Haiku in this book are the 70 that I consider the best (and least moany) of the 150 that I wrote in 36 days.

Where I work, you're not allowed to learn anything; you're expected to know it by default.

"Can you 3D CAD?"
"Nope, never used it before."
"You have an hour; learn!"

However, they were very gracious, and allowed me an entire hour to learn how to use a professional 3D modelling software.

We have a small pond/fountain in our entrance hall, and for reasons completely unknown to me, there are fish in it. I can think of no possible reason for there to be fish there.

There's fish in the pond.
They are underdeveloped.
They are our mascots.

At least the fish know our plight; doomed to mill around, never going anywhere. I guess that's why I get on so well with them.

I'm glad that I have a manager that takes my professional development seriously. It's great to have someone who's there to push you to your limits.

"Training course for you!"
"When?" "Never, I was joking."
"Oh, okay then, thanks...?"

Oh well, then. I guess I'll just find some online courses to complete in my own time, **and add them to my CV!**

"Dear sir, I would like to attend a training course, specifically *<this training course>*, to allow me to carry out my role more efficiently."

Others get training.
But I've noticed that I don't.
Why is this? "Because."

"Hahahahahahahaha! You don't get training."

My organisation has an interesting method of determining if someone is capable for a specific job.

All I need to do.
Is this complex process twice.
And I am adroit?

Essentially, they have to be observed carrying out the job correctly twice, and then they are considered masters and are certified as capable (regardless of the complexity of the task). Hooray for arbitrary criteria that satisfy quality management legislation!

07

On Professional Engineering

I am a professional engineer, but I am not a Professional Engineer. My company has kindly informed me that they expect me to become a licensed PE. They are very, very funny.

After being notified of my company's expectations for me, and once I had finally contained my laughter, I enquired as to how my role would change following the gaining of a license.

"How will my role change.
When I become licensed, sir?
It won't? Oh... okay..."

I didn't expect much, but I didn't expect that there would be no change whatsoever.

I'm firmly of the belief that it's not possible for me to become licensed in the role I currently hold.

I will be PE.
And a master of odd-jobs.
A true Engineer!

For instance (and as far as I am aware), there's no call for Professional Odd-Job Engineers. Yet...

I'm glad that I'm not a licensed Professional Engineer.

When I am PE.
It will be disappointing
For all Engineers.

First of all, I would never trust another Professional Engineer ever again. And, secondly, there would surely be an outcry and widespread protest amongst all Professional Engineers.

08

On Salespeople...

Inevitably, when you're employed as an engineer, you're going to meet salespeople. You don't have to like it, you just have to deal with it. Even worse, though, is when you have to be the salesperson. But, those terrors are for another book.

Nothing builds trust like a broken promise.

Salesman came in here.
He said he would take bagels.
He was a liar...

And nothing is exactly what he took.

More broken promises!

Salesperson visits:
"You'll have your quote
tomorrow."
Quote arrived: never.

Hopefully, their next day delivery isn't the same...

09

On Working Conditions

This chapter is dedicated to the wonderful working world we work in. Here, working conditions can be either physical conditions (such as the blazing heat being channelled directly from the molten core of the earth into my cubicle), or emotional conditions (such as the crushing despair I experience on a daily basis).

We start with a bittersweet Haiku;

My chair is broken.
Just like my spirit is crushed.
Oh well, it's pay day.

Whilst it is true that my spirit is crushed and that my chair is not functioning as it should be, I do have a job that I'm massively thankful for. It may not sound like it within this book, but I am genuinely grateful that I am fortunate enough to have a job.

What's easier to fill, a cup, or a hypothetical motivation receptacle?

My cup sits empty.
Just like my motivation.
I'll feng-shui my desk.

I'm going to go with a cup. I think my motivation receptacle is truly hypothetical. Regardless, rearranging my desk affected neither. I guess I maybe didn't arrange it correctly. I'll try again tomorrow.

It can get pretty warm in a windowless box.

Temperature: Soaring.
The work I'm doing: Boring.
Soon, I'll be: Snoring.

I may invest in several thousand heatsinks and thermal paste, and stick them to every available surface. Or another fan, a fan might work better.

There are several interesting effects of working without exposure to natural light.

My face, it does burn;
Outside, where there is sunlight.
Inside, there is none.

One is instant skin conflagration upon exposure to ultraviolet light. At least it isn't an issue in the winter, when I only see the sun at the weekends.

Let us depart from this subject with a paraphrased quote from my CEO.

"A waste of money.
Is *exactly* what you are."
Says the CEO

This is only minimally paraphrased, the exact quote is "You are an absolute waste of money." But that had too many syllables. To this day, I still don't know if he was joking. I expect he was, as I'm still employed.

10

On Financial Matters

Financial Matters. Whilst the world of finance is abundant in maths (and my job isn't), I do struggle to take any interest in it. However, I do realise that it's of critical importance to my continued employment, and the following Haiku convey some of my more memorable brushes with Financial Matters.

I really respect the ability of my manager to bump prices up.

"We lost 10 cent screw.
Can we get a new one, please?"
"90 dollars, please."

I would never have the courage to attempt a mark-up of that magnitude.

Despite my manager's ability to bump up prices, he emphaticallybelieves that other companies are not allowed to do anything of the sort.

"I want it cheaper.
Tell them I want it cheaper.
Then, ask for discount!"

If no discounts are given, alternative sources must be found and utilized wherever possible.

11

On Communication (and Lack Thereof)

I dislike communication, as it invariably ends up with me receiving horrendously terrible jobs that are awful. Things like "Count the number of things in the thing" and "Ask these people why it costs money for them to send these things to us!" However, I also like communication. For example, it would be nice to hear "We're still making enough money to not fire you all" every so often.

I've been dreaming of efficient ways to deal with the emails I receive.

Emails, oh Emails!
Press Control, A and Delete.
And now they are gone.

This was the best way.

There's always a very tense moment in the morning whilst my computer is awakening. There's an ominous, looming feeling that I've actually received a generous quantity of work (which, in itself, would not be a bad thing); but, work so dull that counting individual vaporizing water molecules escaping from liquid paint would seem wildly engrossing.

The day has begun.
No emails came overnight.
Thank goodness for that.

But, alas! No work appears. Not even a single mind-numbingly tedious task! Whilst the relief is great at this revelation. The full consequences eventually settle in; I have no work again...

Then, SUDDENLY, and after weeks of odd-jobs (and halfway through the afternoon), my manager appears with an engineering job!

"I have been meaning.
To give you this job for weeks.
Need it done today."

A job that has been withheld for weeks and is due today? Lucky Me!

12

On the Wonder of Spreadsheets

Spreadsheets are the only constantly present part of my job. Well, you know, apart from all the odd-jobs and crushing despair.

Spreadsheets have many uses, and are nearly omnipresent in my workplace.

Spreadsheets always there.
Like another limb for me.
I am Engineer.

They are my friends.

Every so often, an ill-constructed macro runs amok and eats my data, or reduces it to an unusable mass of smouldering runes.

Big macro mishap.
All my data is now gone.
Oh no! Start again.

Naturally, it's entirely my fault. But, at least I can roll-back to the previous save. Incidentally, this has taught me to save often, and in multiple files

I once created a most wondrous spreadsheet. In which, there was a column of several thousand cells that each contained a 3662 character expression.

IF AND AND IF OR
AND OR X3=2.
Spreadsheet Logic Fun.

There were many AND/OR/IF statements, and many levels of nesting.

13

On the Management of Projects

I don't manage projects anymore; as there are no projects for me to manage. But, I have been part of many projects, and many seem to have a similar theme.

The recurring theme that I have noticed goes like this;

Interesting job.
At last, is bestowed on me.
Oh, wait, it's cancelled...

The first few times, I found it mildly frustrating.

The following few times, my feelings intensified.

Working on a good job.
And then, just like a whirlwind.
Job cancelled again.

On these occasions, I felt mildly infuriated.

Now, I just expect every project to end at any moment.

Approved, then cancelled.
Then approved, and then cancelled.
Approved, then cancelled.

Sometimes, I've found, a project can end more than once. They may reappear and disappear at will!

14

On The End of the Day

Ah! The end of the day! A time of joy!

Until someone cheerily says "See you tomorrow!" Or, worse, "See you in 16 hours!" Those people are the worst. I didn't really have an issue with the phrase "See you tomorrow" until I realised that I didn't want to see them tomorrow, as that meant that I would be back in the office.

At this point in the day, there isn't really any time left to engage in any productive work.

Three minutes to go.
Close all except one spreadsheet.
(Looks like I'm working)

So, you open a spreadsheet, and scroll blankly through the data. You can't possibly not be working if you have a spreadsheet in front of you.

I'm always ready for 17:00! Just as the second hand lands on the 12, I'm immediately closing down everything, and the PC follows shortly after.

The clock, it does strike.
And, I am out of the door.
Before the fifth one.

Out the door, down the elevator, on the bus. In one fluid movement.

There is relief on a Friday when I leave work. I know there's only 63 hours until I return, but they will be an excellent 63 hours where I will not think about the office.

Today is Friday.
And my spirits are lifted.
Until Sunday night.

Until Sunday night, when I'm full of dread for the coming Monday again...

15

On A Miscellanea of Subjects

This chapter contains, as you'd expect, Haiku of miscellaneous subject matter.

The only part of QC I am glad of, is the sample set part. It's a wonderful loophole that allows for the dimensional checking of 1,000 items, out of a 10,000 item order.

"Did you check them all?"
"I checked 10% of them"
"That is close enough."

If 10% are acceptable, all are acceptable. If 10% are unacceptable, pick another 10%. Just kidding, that would be unethical.

Certain incorrect, but commonly-used, terms annoy me immeasurably.

"Did you say 'Wattage?'
Do you say 'Fahrenheitage?'
Or, perhaps, 'Ohmage?' "

I do not handle their use as well as I could. I tend to 'overreact,' according to some sources[1].

[1]Apparently, extrapolating the inappropriate use of the suffix '-age' to other words in return conversage is not professional behavage

I am occasionally told to 'think outside the box', 'be creative', 'use initiative', or to 'use this example as an example'.

"Use initiative"
Is what he said; so I did.
Won't do that again...

It usually results in me being questioned as to why I decided to do things differently, or being reprimanded for making my work 'too different' from the example.

’Twas the end of the meeting, and all through the hall.
Not a person was conscious; not any, at all.

This meeting will test.
The limits of your patience.
And resisting sleep.

So many were there, but only in body. Most fell asleep,
’cause the presenter was shoddy.

I always have this naïve hope that I'm going to return to work from a vacation, and find that I have some wonderful engineering work to do.

Back from vacation.
It's worse now than when I left.
More vacation, please.

It's never the case...

Let's end the miscellanea on a serious note.

The scariest phrase.
That I've heard in my career:
"We are downsizing."

And this is exactly why I'm extremely thankful for my job,

16

I'll Emphasise This One

Work before family.
Is what's expected of me.
Hahahaha no...

17

Bonus Tanka

Job satisfaction?
Ha ha ha ha ha ha ha!
Ha ha ha ha ha!
Ha ha ha ha ha ha ha!
Ha ha ha ha ha ha ha!

18

A Goodbye, of Sorts

To whom it may concern,

Thank you for reading my book. Or, at the very least, thank you for looking at this page of my book, and I suggest you read the pages prior to this. I really hope that you've enjoyed my book, and that you weren't able to relate to every Haiku within. This book was an incredible vent of my frustration and it was a great feeling to see it come together, as I don't often see anything come of my work.

I would also like to take this opportunity to point out that, despite the impressive levels of moaning that I have achieved within this book, I am actually massively thankful for my job. I realise that I am truly blessed to have a job that allows me to provide for my family.

I wish you all the very best within your career, be you at the start, middle or end. Additionally, I really hope that I haven't put anyone off a career in Engineering; just be sure that you pick a good company. I'm sure that my experiences are the exception, rather than the norm.

Goodbye to you all.
But, while this book has ended;
Oh, there may be more...

Thanks for reading,
Pip Merryweather.

A

Statistics

This chapter is dedicated entirely to statistics about the book. I'm sure that the more inquisitive amongst you have had unanswered questions all the way through. Possibly, you're curious as to how many Syllables are present within the Haiku? You may wonder how many characters are present within the Haiku? It may be that you want to know the average number of syllables per word? Or, perhaps you don't...

Anyway, these are the kinds of things I get curious about;

- The Haiku in this book (outwith the introduction and conclusion);
  - Consist of 1,224 Syllables
  - Consist of 902 words (416 unique words),
  - Consist of 5,612 characters, excluding punctuation (but including apostrophes).
  - Have a mean syllable per word value of 1.35698.
  - Have a mean character per syllable value of 4.58497.
  - Contain an average of 12.8857 Words.

Interestingly, the average word per Haiku is roughly equal to 4π, which led me down an interesting path:

$$12.8857 - 4\pi \approx \frac{\pi}{10} + 1.6457004\%$$

$$1.6457004 \approx \frac{1+\sqrt{5}}{2} + 0.0276641$$

$$0.0276641 \approx \frac{e^1}{100} + 0.000483591$$

and, if an electromagnetic wave had a wavelength of 0.000483591 mm (483 nm), it would be a nice shade of cyan.

Index of Despair

www.ingramcontent.com/pod-product-compliance
Lightning Source LLC
Chambersburg PA
CBHW050957050726
47592CB00007B/2606

* 9 7 8 1 7 8 8 0 8 1 6 9 6 *